HENRY VIII
AND HIS SIX WIVES

King Henry the Eighth of England was famous for many things, but he was also famous because he had six wives. He was not a kind husband. People say that when he was looking for a new wife, careful fathers took their daughters away from the palace. They did not want the King to choose their daughter to be the next Queen, because some of his Queens had very short and unhappy lives.

Why did King Henry divorce two wives, and kill two others? What were his queens really like?

Catherine Parr, the sixth wife, lived on after the King's death. One day she goes back to the palace of Whitehall and finds a box of old letters written to the King – one from each of the first five wives. She sits down to read them to her young maid, Margaret. The first letter is from the daughter of the King of Spain, Katherine of Aragon, who was Henry's wife for twenty-four years. She died alone and sad and friendless . . .

OXFORD BOOKWORMS LIBRARY
True Stories

Henry VIII and his Six Wives

Stage 2 (700 headwords)

Series Editor: Jennifer Bassett
Founder Editor: Tricia Hedge
Activities Editors: Jennifer Bassett and Alison Baxter

JANET HARDY-GOULD

Henry VIII
and his Six Wives

OXFORD UNIVERSITY PRESS

OXFORD
UNIVERSITY PRESS

Great Clarendon Street, Oxford OX2 6DP

Oxford University Press is a department of the University of Oxford.
It furthers the University's objective of excellence in research, scholarship,
and education by publishing worldwide in

Oxford New York

Auckland Cape Town Dar es Salaam Hong Kong Karachi
Kuala Lumpur Madrid Melbourne Mexico City Nairobi
New Delhi Shanghai Taipei Toronto

With offices in

Argentina Austria Brazil Chile Czech Republic France Greece
Guatemala Hungary Italy Japan Poland Portugal Singapore
South Korea Switzerland Thailand Turkey Ukraine Vietnam

ISBN-13: 978 0 19 422975 3
ISBN-10: 0 19 422975 0

Printed in Hong Kong

ACKNOWLEDGEMENTS

Original illustrations by: Richard Allen

The publishers would like to thank

the following for their permission to reproduce illustrations:

The Bridgeman Art Library p 19, 24; His Grace the Archbishop of Canterbury p 36;
The Hulton Deutsch Collection Limited p 34; National Portrait Gallery p 3, 7, 12;
The Royal Collection © Her Majesty Queen Elizabeth II p 29

CONTENTS

1

King Henry is dead

My name is Catherine Parr. A month ago I was the Queen of England, the wife of King Henry the Eighth. Henry died and we buried him last week in St George's Church, Windsor. Two days ago, on 16th February 1547, I went back to the palace of Whitehall, which was once my home. I wanted to take my letters and books and bring them back to my house.

Margaret, my new maid, came to the palace with me. She's very young and doesn't know a lot about the world. She has only just come up to London from her home in Somerset. Perhaps I was like her when I was twelve. I, too,

Two days ago I went back to the palace of Whitehall.

was always asking questions and wanting answers immediately.

When we arrived at the palace, it was cold and dark. We walked into Henry's room. I sat down in one of Henry's large chairs in front of his wooden writing desk and looked at the pictures around the room. Next to me there was a big picture of Henry, when he was young. He was very handsome then, not like the fat old man he was later. I thought his blue eyes were watching me. I turned to Margaret and said:

'You see that picture of the King? That's what he was like when he was young – tall and strong and handsome. People say that he never got tired. He could go out riding all day, changing his horses nine or ten times, and then he could dance all night. He was clever, too; he could speak five languages. Will people remember him like that, or will they only remember him because he had six wives?'

'Did he really have so many wives?' said Margaret.

'Yes, of course. I thought that everyone knew that.'

Margaret looked away and said, 'We didn't get much news from London at home, and my family's house is a long way from the nearest village.'

'It doesn't matter,' I said, smiling. 'One day, I'll tell you the story of my husband Henry's life.'

On the desk in front of me there was a wooden box with a large gold H on the top. I opened it slowly and took out some old letters. Each letter was in different writing

*'That's what the King was like when he was young
– tall and strong and handsome.'*

and some of them were old and yellow. One letter had a picture of a large bird on it. It was from Henry's second wife, Anne Boleyn.

'Margaret!' I said. 'I've found some letters from Henry's other wives. There's also a beautiful gold necklace and a small piece of hair.' I looked at another letter. 'Here's one old letter from his first wife, Katherine of Aragon. She was married to him for a very long time.'

'She only had one child, didn't she?' said Margaret.

'Yes, only Princess Mary is still alive. There were five other children, but they were all born too early and died.'

Again I looked at the letter with the picture of the bird on it. 'Have you heard of Anne Boleyn, Margaret?'

'Yes, my mother talked about her. She said she was a very bad woman.'

'Well, that's what some people say. Anne was the mother of Henry's second daughter, Princess Elizabeth. Look,' I said. 'This one is from Katherine Howard, Henry's fifth wife. Both Anne and Katherine were beheaded in that terrible prison, the Tower of London.'

'Why did the King send them to their deaths?' asked Margaret. She looked afraid.

'They had many enemies, who told the King that they had lovers. Perhaps the stories were true, I don't know. But the King believed them.'

I looked at another letter. 'This one is from Jane Seymour. She was the third wife and the mother of Henry's only living son. He is now our King, Edward the Sixth.'

'Was Jane Seymour beheaded too?' asked Margaret.

'No, poor Queen Jane died soon after Edward was born.'

I looked at the last, short letter. 'Look, a letter from Anne of Cleves, Henry's fourth wife.'

'Did she have any children?' asked Margaret.

'No,' I laughed. 'Henry thought that Anne was very ugly and he didn't want her to be the mother of his children.'

Margaret was silent. Then she said, 'King Henry sounds like a terrible husband.'

'He wasn't all bad, Margaret. There were good times, too. He was clever at so many things – horse-riding and tennis, writing and playing music. He wrote many beautiful songs, and he had a wonderful singing voice. But it's true that he wasn't very kind to his wives.'

Margaret looked at the box. 'So why did he keep these letters from them?' she asked.

'Oh, you ask so many questions, Margaret! I don't know. Perhaps each letter says something important.'

I looked up and saw that it was nearly dark. It was time to go home to Chelsea Manor. I put the letters back inside the box.

'Come, Margaret, we must go now.'

'But can't we read the letters?' she asked.

'We'll take them with us and read them tomorrow.'

There were some letters from Henry's wives in the box.

2

Katherine of Aragon

We got up early the next morning and went to my favourite room. It has a wonderful view of the large gardens and the River Thames at the bottom.

'Did you sleep well, Margaret?' I asked.

'No. I dreamed that King Henry came back to life and sent me to the Tower of London.'

'Why did he do that?'

'Because in my dream I read the letters and he was angry with me. Perhaps it will be bad luck if we read them,' said Margaret, worried.

'Don't worry,' I said. 'It was only a dream. He can't do anything now. He's dead.'

I went over to the wooden box and opened it. 'We'll read the letter from Katherine of Aragon first,' I said.

'She was Spanish, wasn't she?' said Margaret.

'Yes, she first came over to England to marry Henry's brother Arthur, but he died. She then married Henry and was his wife and queen for twenty-four years.'

'What a long time! What happened to her? Did she go to the Tower of London too?'

'No, Henry divorced Katherine because he wanted a son, and she only gave him a daughter, Princess Mary. Years before, Katherine *did* have a son – Henry, Prince of Wales,

*'Katherine of Aragon was Henry's wife and queen
for twenty-four years.'*

but he died when he was only seven weeks old. The King
wanted a son very much. He was in love with Anne Boleyn,
but he also wanted a new wife – a younger woman to give
him sons.'

'Poor Katherine! Divorced after twenty-four years for a

younger woman!' Margaret looked at the letter in my hand.
'Can we read the letter now, my lady?'

'Yes, let's sit down by the window and read it together.'

'But I can't read,' said Margaret, looking at the floor.

'That's all right, I'll read it for you.'

We sat down and I began to read it slowly . . .

Windsor

28th July 1531

Dear Henry

When you left Windsor last week, you didn't say
goodbye. I feel lonely and unhappy without you. When
will I see you again? Please come back soon.

You know that I am your true wife. We have been
married for more than twenty years in the eyes of God.
I have given you a daughter, Princess Mary. God took
from us our other children. I wanted so much to give
you a son, but God's plan for us was different, and we
cannot change that.

I pray for you every day and ask for you to come back
to me. I have never been untrue to you, Henry, and have
always been a good wife, and a good mother to our
daughter.

I am still your Queen. There is only one Queen of
England, and that is me. I know that you are with Anne
Boleyn, but you will never be happy with her. I am the
daughter of a King, and she is not. You must not divorce

me. The Pope and the Catholic Church will never agree
to this. I am sending you a necklace with a gold cross.
Henry, when you look at it, remember me and remember
the Catholic Church.

> Your Queen
> Katherine of Aragon

'So what happened to Katherine?' asked Margaret. 'Did
she ever see the King again?'

'No, never. He divorced her. She lived a lonely life with
only a few friends, and died a broken and unhappy woman
about ten years ago.'

'What about the Catholic Church? Did the Pope agree
to the divorce?'

'No, he didn't. So Henry broke with the Pope and the
Catholic Church, and that's how the Church of England
began. The King became Head of the Church, and the Pope
and the Catholics were very angry. It made a lot of trouble
both in England and Europe.'

'And all because of Anne Boleyn?' said Margaret.

'Not only that. You see, it was very important for the
King to have a son, to be King after him. There has only
ever been one Queen in England, and that was a terrible
time, with a lot of fighting and killing. Henry didn't want
that to happen again after his death. So he knew that he
must have a son, not just daughters. And that's really why
he divorced Katherine and married again.'

'And was he sad when Katherine died?'

'Sad? Oh no! He dressed in yellow and danced all night with his new Queen.'

Margaret looked inside the box and found the gold necklace. She held it to her neck. 'Poor Katherine,' she said softly. 'King Henry was a terrible husband to her.'

*'The King dressed in yellow and danced all night
with his new Queen.'*

3

Anne Boleyn

Margaret carefully put the necklace back into the box, then looked at me.

'So then the King married Anne Boleyn,' she said. 'Was Anne very special? Was she really very beautiful?'

'Some people say that she was, and others say that she wasn't. But she had beautiful long black hair, and the most wonderful black eyes. When men looked into her eyes, they fell in love with her.'

'Tell me more about her,' said Margaret.

'Well, Henry was in love with her for about seven years before they married.'

'Seven years!'

'Yes, it took a long time to divorce Katherine, and Anne wanted to marry the King and be his Queen. She didn't want to be just his mistress, like the other girls.'

'Did the King have a lot of mistresses?' asked Margaret. Her eyes were round with interest.

'Oh yes,' I said, smiling. 'Kings can do what they like, you know. But people say that Anne was very clever. She said no to the King, again and again, and so he had to marry her to get what he wanted.'

'And how long were they married?'

'Less than three and a half years.'

'People say that Anne Boleyn was very clever.'

'Is that all?' said Margaret. 'King Henry broke with the Pope to marry Anne, and they were only married for three and a half years!'

'Yes, Henry soon became tired of her. He wanted a son, but she only gave him a daughter, Princess Elizabeth. She nearly had another baby, but she had a miscarriage after only a few months. They could see that it was a boy. Henry was very, very angry, and three months later Anne was in the Tower of London. Henry was already interested in Jane Seymour, you see.'

'So poor Anne went to the Tower because she didn't give the King a son?'

'Well, there were other things. Anne was a strong and sometimes difficult woman. She talked a lot. She liked to tell Henry what to do. In the end Henry became bored of this. Remember, he was the King of England.'

'Did she really have lovers?'

'Well, some people say—'

Just then there was a noise outside. I looked out of the window and saw a man on a horse. He had grey hair and was wearing fine clothes. It was my Uncle William. A minute later he came into the room.

'Hello,' I said, kissing him. 'I'm so pleased to see you.'

'Dear Catherine,' he said. 'It's wonderful to see you, too. And who is this?' he said, turning to Margaret.

'I'm Margaret, my lady's new maid.'

'I'm very pleased to meet you,' he said, smiling. 'So,' he went on, 'what's the news?'

'Oh, we were just talking about Anne Boleyn,' I said.

'That black-eyed witch!' said Uncle William.

'Was she really a witch?' asked Margaret.

'Well, she was a strange woman,' said Uncle William. 'She had six fingers on one hand. I saw them myself.

Witches always have six fingers. Anne Boleyn was a wild and dangerous woman – but men liked her.'

'So she did have lovers, then?' said Margaret.

'Of course she did!' said Uncle William. 'There were five of them – all wild young men. They were all beheaded before the witch, and a good thing too!'

'Oh, Uncle,' I said, 'how can we be sure that they were all her lovers? One of them was her brother!'

'Well, perhaps *he* wasn't her lover,' said Uncle William.

'They were all beheaded before the witch – and a good thing too!'

'But I remember all those wild parties in the Queen's rooms. There was dancing and laughing all night sometimes. She was a bad woman, I'm sure of it.'

'I think that Henry believed the stories about Anne because he wanted another wife,' I said. 'A wife to give him a son.'

Little Margaret was listening to us with great interest. 'So nobody was sorry when Anne died?' she said.

'No, many people were pleased,' said Uncle William. 'She had a lot of enemies.' Then he looked at both of us. 'But why are you talking about Anne Boleyn? That's very old news.'

'I found this old box of Henry's at Whitehall Palace,' I said. 'Inside there were letters from each of Henry's wives, and Margaret wanted to know all about them.'

'Where's the one from Anne Boleyn?' said Uncle William. He opened the box on the table. 'I want to read what she wrote to her dear husband. Ah, here it is. 18th May 1536 – that's the day before she was beheaded.'

He began to read the letter aloud . . .

Tower of London
18th May 1536

Dear Henry
This is my last letter to you. Tomorrow I am going to die. When you open this letter and read it, I will be dead and buried.

During the last few weeks my life has been very hard. I have been very afraid and very lonely. I have walked around my room, thinking of you. I wanted you to take me away from this terrible prison. But now I know that I am going to die, I feel calm.

They tell me that you have spoken angry words about me. You say I have had a hundred lovers, not just the five poor men who have died because of me.

But I did not have lovers, Henry. Not one, and you know it. I was a true wife to you, but you listened to my enemies, and that is why I am here.

I ask one last thing. Please be kind to our daughter Elizabeth. Do not be angry with *her*, because of *me*. She is so very young, not yet three years old. I am sending a gold necklace to give to her. It will help her to remember me.

I have only a little neck, so it will not be difficult for the French sword to cut through it tomorrow.

Tonight I will pray for God to forgive you.

> Your wife
> Anne Boleyn

'And was Anne beheaded the next day?' asked Margaret.

'Yes,' I said. 'With a sword. That's how they do it in France.'

'How terrible!' said Margaret, holding her neck.

'Well, I know that Henry did the right thing,' said Uncle

William. 'Anne Boleyn was no good. She wasn't a real Queen. Not like Katherine of Aragon.' He stood up. 'I must go,' he said. 'This is all very interesting, but I came here to talk to your brother. I'll go and find him. Goodbye for now, ladies.' He smiled and left the room.

'Where's the necklace?' asked Margaret.

'I can't find it,' I said, looking in the box. 'Perhaps Henry gave it to Princess Elizabeth. Perhaps she looks at it sometimes and thinks of her mother.'

'Perhaps Henry gave the necklace to Princess Elizabeth.'

4

Jane Seymour

P eople say that Princess Elizabeth is very clever,' said
Margaret. 'Is that true, my lady?'

'Yes, it is. She's only thirteen years old, but she can read
and write in four languages already.'

Margaret's face was sad. 'I only know *one* language,'
she said. 'And I can't read *or* write it.'

'But you have a mother and father who are alive,' I said
quickly. 'You don't have enemies who watch you all the
time, or who want to send you far away to marry a stranger
– perhaps an old man who drinks too much, and keeps a
mistress!'

'Will that happen to Princess Elizabeth?' Margaret
asked, her eyes round.

'Perhaps. Who knows? A princess doesn't always have
an easy life, you know.' I laughed. 'But Elizabeth is clever.
I think she'll get what she wants in life. Now, let's go
outside, while the sun is shining. We'll take the next letter
with us.'

We walked down through the garden to the river. There
we sat on a seat and watched the boats.

'So Jane Seymour was the third wife,' said Margaret.
'When did the King marry her?'

'Just ten days after Anne's death.'

'Jane Seymour was quiet and careful.'

'That was very quick!'

'Yes, Henry always knew what he wanted. And he usually wanted things immediately.'

'And was Jane the same as Anne Boleyn?'

'No, Jane was very different. She was quiet and careful. Before she married the King, she was never alone with him. Her brother Edward was always with her when the King came to visit. And Henry was pleased to see that. He didn't want another wild and dangerous wife like Anne.'

'How do you know so much about the King and his other wives?' asked Margaret.

'I have lived for many years in palaces, Margaret,' I said,

smiling. 'And palaces are full of people, coming and going, talking in corners, telling secrets. If you listen, it's not difficult to learn things.'

'So was Jane a nicer person than Anne?'

'Palaces are full of people, coming and going, talking in corners, telling secrets.'

'I think she was. She was very kind to Henry's daughters, Princess Mary and Princess Elizabeth. She was like a mother to both of them. Jane was clever too, and she quickly learnt to listen to Henry. She didn't try to tell him what to do. And with her brown hair and white face, she also looked very different to Anne Boleyn.'

'And what about the King at this time? Was he still handsome?'

'Oh no, he was beginning to get fat and his face was just like a big potato! Not like the picture in Whitehall Palace.'

'But was he happy?' asked Margaret.

'Yes, I think he really loved Jane. And of course, she also gave him a baby boy, who is now our King Edward.'

'A son at last for the King! But what happened to Jane? Did he get tired of her too, or was she the one who died?'

'Yes, she died soon after Edward was born.'

'How sad! She gave the King a son and then she died.'

'Let's read the letter now.' I opened it and a piece of brown hair fell out. I showed it to Margaret.

'What soft hair,' she said, touching it. 'Is it Jane's?'

'Yes, I think so.' I began to read . . .

Hampton Court Palace
22nd October 1537

Dear Henry
The doctors and my women tell me that I shall feel better tomorrow, but I can see in their faces that it is not true.

I cannot sleep or eat, and a fire burns in my body day and night. I know that I shall soon be dead.

But I have given you a son, Henry, and I can die happy, knowing that Edward will be King after you. I will never see the day when he becomes King, but I pray that God will give him a long and happy life.

Please look after dear Edward and tell him all about me. Here is a piece of my hair – a small present from a dying mother to her baby son.

I am too ill to write more and must say goodbye.

Your loving wife and queen

Jane

I put the letter away, and looked at Margaret. 'She had a very difficult time when the baby was born, you see. It took three days and two nights before the baby arrived. Poor Jane was very tired and ill. She died twelve days later, very soon after this letter.'

'How terrible,' said Margaret. She touched the piece of Jane's hair again. 'And was the King sad?'

'Oh yes. He was very unhappy. He shut himself away in the palace for weeks. All England was sad, and every church in the country said prayers for poor Queen Jane. She was buried at Windsor, and Henry is now buried next to her.'

Just then Uncle William came up behind us.

'Ah, Uncle,' I said. 'Let's go in and have some lunch.'

5

Anne of Cleves

After lunch we sat and talked for a while. Uncle William was very interested in the letters.

'So which letter are you going to read next?' he asked.

'The one from Anne of Cleves,' I replied.

'Oh yes, Henry's ugly wife. When I first saw her, I thought she looked just like a horse! And the King thought that too!'

'A horse?' said Margaret. 'So how did she become the King's wife?'

'It's a long story. Do you want to hear it?'

'Yes, please,' said Margaret, smiling.

'Well, after poor Queen Jane died, Henry was very sad and lonely. He wanted a new wife, and he wanted a second son. Children can die at any time, and Edward wasn't strong. So everybody looked for a beautiful young woman to be the new Queen. Then someone told Henry about Anne of Cleves, a German Princess. They said that she was beautiful, young, and clever. And at that time the King wanted to please the Germans, because he was angry with the French. That all changed later, of course.

'Henry couldn't go and see Anne for himself, so he sent his artist Holbein to paint a picture of her. Holbein painted a fine picture of Anne and sent it back to Henry. Henry

'Holbein painted a fine picture of Anne of Cleves.'

immediately fell in love with the beautiful woman in the
picture and decided to marry her. So Anne sailed to
England, and on her way to London she stopped for the
night at a small town called Rochester. Henry couldn't wait
for Anne to arrive in London so he travelled secretly to

Rochester to meet her. She knew nothing about this.

'When Henry arrived at her house, he wasn't wearing his fine clothes and he didn't look like a king. He knocked on the door and went into her room. Oh dear! Poor Henry was very surprised. This wasn't the beautiful woman in the picture. She had a sad face and a long nose, and she wasn't very interested in this strange man. He didn't tell her his name, and she didn't understand that this was her new husband. What a terrible mistake!

'Poor Henry went away to put on his fine clothes, and came back looking like a real king. Anne now saw that this strange man was her new husband. Henry kissed Anne and said his name. Poor Anne smiled at him, but she couldn't speak any English so she stayed silent. After a few minutes Henry left. He was really unhappy. His new wife wasn't beautiful, and she couldn't say a word to him!'

'Oh dear,' said Margaret. She was enjoying this story very much. 'What happened next?'

'Well, Henry decided that he really didn't want to marry Anne. Where was the beautiful young woman in the picture? He wanted *her*! But he couldn't change things. He had to marry ugly Anne.'

'And did the King learn to love her?' asked Margaret.

'No, he didn't. He wanted to divorce her.'

'And did he?'

'Yes, after six months.'

'How did he do that?'

'Well, he learned that in her country Anne was engaged at one time to marry another man.'

'And so he divorced her?'

'Yes, poor Anne was only Queen for six months.'

'And they didn't have any children, did they?'

'No, Henry didn't sleep with Anne.'

'But what happened to her? Is she still alive?'

'Oh yes. But let's read her letter and see what she says.'

'Perhaps it's a love letter,' said Margaret.

'If it is, I'm sure that she never got a reply!' said Uncle William, laughing. He opened the letter and began to read.

Palace of Richmond

20th July 1540

Dear Henry

You are a very good brother to me! Thank you for giving me five hundred pounds a year and the Palace of Richmond. I spend hours walking round the gardens here – the trees and flowers are wonderful.

I have decided that I shall not go back to my country. I have thought about it carefully, and I know now that England is my real home. I feel so happy here. How can I leave all my dear English friends and my beautiful garden?

Come and visit me soon, dear brother.

Your loving sister

Anne

'She sounds really happy,' said Margaret, surprised.

'I think she is,' said Uncle William. 'She didn't make trouble for the King about her divorce, so he was pleased with her. And then, of course, he was free to marry his next wife.'

'The fifth one,' said Margaret. 'And who was she?'

'Catherine will tell you all about her. I must leave you now, ladies.' He stood up, and came to kiss me goodbye.

'Goodbye, Uncle,' I said. 'Come again soon.'

'Oh, I will. I'd like to read the rest of those letters.' He looked at Margaret. 'Be good, young lady.' He smiled at us both and left the room.

'I spend hours walking round the gardens here.'

6

Katherine Howard

I took the last letter out of the box and held it in my
hand while I answered Margaret's questions. She
wanted to know everything.

'And who was the King's fifth wife?' she asked.

'Katherine Howard.'

'Why did the King want to marry again?'

'He still wanted to have another son, you see. A brother
for Prince Edward.'

'And how did he meet Katherine?' asked Margaret.

'She was one of the ladies at Queen Anne's palace, so
Henry knew her already. She was only eighteen. Henry
fell in love with her immediately. He called her "his
beautiful flower" and sent her many expensive presents –
gold and jewels and fine dresses.'

'But did she want to marry him?'

I smiled. 'If the King of England wants to marry you,
how do you say no? Henry was very much in love and he
wanted to marry her immediately. The Howard family is
an old and famous one, and they were very happy for
Katherine to marry the King.'

'Was he happy with his new Queen?'

'Yes,' I said. 'At first. She was young, beautiful, and
exciting. Very different from Anne of Cleves.'

'Henry was very much in love with Katherine Howard.'

'And did she learn to love the King?'

'Who can say? But I don't think so. Henry was forty-nine, thirty years older than her. He was very, very fat and heavy. His face was more like a potato than ever, and his eyes were always half-closed. He had a very bad leg and often couldn't walk – and he was always angry when his leg hurt.'

Margaret looked at the letter in my hand. 'I don't think that I would like to marry a fat old man with a bad leg who couldn't walk!' she said.

I laughed. 'But the King's wife, remember, was also the Queen of England, the first lady in the country.'

'Yes, that's true,' said Margaret. 'And did they have a son?'

'No, they didn't. They weren't married for very long. Before Katherine married Henry, she had lovers. Henry didn't know this. He thought that *he* was Katherine's first lover. And about six months after Katherine married Henry, she began to see another man called Thomas Culpeper. He was tall and handsome. Katherine wrote love letters to him, and they met secretly at night.'

'What a dangerous thing to do!' said Margaret.

'Katherine wasn't very clever, I'm afraid.'

'And people saw her and began to talk about it, and somebody told the King . . .'

'One of his friends wrote it all down in a letter, and put the letter into Henry's hand when he was in church.'

'Oh dear,' said Margaret. 'So then . . .' Already she knew what happened next.

'Yes,' I said. 'Henry was wildly angry. He talked, people say, about taking a sword and cutting off her head himself. But he sent Thomas Culpeper to prison, and soon after he sent Katherine to the Tower.'

'Like Anne Boleyn, years before,' said Margaret.

'Katherine met Thomas Culpeper secretly at night.'

'Let's see what her letter says,' I said, opening it. 'The writing is very untidy – I think she wrote this in a hurry.'

Tower of London
11th February 1541

Dear Henry
Please forgive me! I didn't want to make you unhappy and angry. Believe me!

It's true that when I was a young girl, I was friendly with different young men. I was so young and stupid. I also spent a lot of time with Thomas Culpeper when I was your wife. But believe me, Henry, I didn't know what I was doing. Remember, I am only twenty years old now. You are so much older than me, and you understand much more about the world.

Please, Henry, please, please help me! Don't send me to my death! I am so afraid here in the Tower – I pray day and night that you will come and take me away. How can you kill your beautiful flower? They tell me that in two days' time they will cut off my head ... Henry, I don't want to die! Please let me live a little longer ... please! Just a few weeks . . . a few days . . . Please, Henry, please ...

> Your unhappy wife
> Katherine Howard

When I finished reading the letter, Margaret was silent. Perhaps she could hear Katherine Howard's cries and see her white face.

I put the letter away, and Margaret looked at me.

'There aren't any more letters, are there?' she said.

'No,' I said. 'That was the last letter.'

7

Catherine Parr

We sat silently for a while. Outside it was beginning to get dark. Margaret looked at the floor, then at her hands, then at the floor again. I waited. I knew what she was thinking. Then suddenly she looked at me, and the questions came all at once.

'How could you do it, my lady? How could you marry that terrible man? Weren't you afraid? Why didn't you hide . . . or . . . or run away?'

I smiled at her. 'Listen to the full story, and then perhaps you'll understand. I was very different to Henry's other wives. I was thirty-one years old and Henry was my third husband. My first two husbands were old men too. They both died and I didn't have any children with them. But Henry didn't really want a wife, Margaret. He wanted a friend, and a nurse, and a mother for his three children.'

'Oh, I see,' said Margaret slowly. 'He wanted someone to look after him. So how did it all happen, then?'

'It began at a party at Hampton Court Palace. I remember it very well. While I was dancing with my friend Thomas Seymour, I turned round and saw Henry. His blue eyes were watching me. He was too ill to dance, but later that evening he asked to talk with me. I was a little afraid. I knew so many different stories about him. He was one of

the most famous kings in Europe, and he was also famous
for killing people who made him angry – Anne Boleyn,
Katherine Howard, and many, many others. And of course,
he was also very fat and ugly!

'How could you marry that terrible man?'

'After that evening he began to send me presents, and
he asked me to visit him at Hampton Court Palace.

'At this time I was friendly with Thomas Seymour. He

was a fine young man and I was in love with him. We talked about getting married. Then I got a letter from King Henry. He wanted to marry me. What could I do? I loved Thomas, but my family wanted me to be the Queen of England. And in the end, I had to marry Henry.'

'But were you happy?' asked Margaret.

'Well, sometimes I was. I loved being Queen. I had beautiful clothes and expensive jewels. But it was also very difficult at times. Henry was often ill with his bad leg, and when his leg hurt, he became angry and shouted at me. Once he nearly sent me to the Tower. I said something about the Church of England, and he didn't agree with me and got very, very angry. He didn't say anything then, but a few days later his soldiers came to take me away.'

'Oh no!' said Margaret. 'What did you do?'

'I cried and cried. I told him that I agreed with his every word, and that he was my teacher and I was only a stupid woman. And then I cried some more, and said I didn't understand anything about the church. I only talked to help him forget his bad leg.'

'And was that true?' asked Margaret.

'Of course not! But I had to say something, and after that we were friends again.'

'So you didn't love him.'

'No, I didn't, but I learned to like him some of the time. He was a clever and interesting man – and he was the King of England!'

'And what about his three children?'

'I felt sorry for them. They had a difficult and lonely life. I tried to be a good mother to them all. I was friendly with Princess Mary, played games with Elizabeth and young Edward, and helped them with their studies in

Catherine Parr

different languages. Of course, Henry and I didn't have any children together.'

Suddenly there was a knock at the door. 'Come in!' I called. A young man walked into the room. He was holding some beautiful red and gold flowers.

'These are for Catherine Parr,' he said.

'For me?' I said. 'Who are they from?'

'There's a note here.' He gave me a piece of paper, smiled, and left the room.

I read the note quickly.

Dear Catherine, you are my true love. You are my flower. I think of you every hour. I wait for you. Tom.

'What does it say?' asked Margaret.

'I can't tell you,' I laughed.

'But who are the flowers from?'

'Thomas Seymour.'

'Oh, the young man who wanted to marry you before. Does he still love you? Are you going to marry him?'

'I don't know, Margaret. Henry only died three weeks ago.' I was silent for a minute, and then I said, 'It's true, I still like Thomas. I often think about him. Some people say he's only interested in two things: women and money. But I don't believe them. He has enemies, you see, because he comes from a famous family. Jane Seymour was his sister, so Thomas is one of King Edward's uncles.'

'Will Edward be a good king, do you think?' asked Margaret.

'These are for Catherine Parr,' the young man said.

'Yes, I think so. He's a very clever child. He often writes me letters in different languages, and he's only nine years old. But I'm worried about him because he's often ill. England needs a strong king. Henry was a bad husband, but he was a strong king of England. If Edward dies, who knows what will happen?'

It was dark outside now. I looked at Margaret and said, 'So, now you have heard all about King Henry and his six wives, and one day you can tell the story to your children and your grandchildren.'

'I think that people will always remember King Henry because of his six wives,' said Margaret. She opened the box and took out the letters. She looked at them, putting them back one by one into the box.

'Divorced – beheaded – died – divorced – beheaded.' She closed the box and looked at me. 'And still alive!'

We both laughed.

'What are you going to do with the letters, my lady?'

'Nothing, Margaret. It will be our secret.'

Catherine Parr married Thomas Seymour in May 1547, a few months after Henry's death. They were married for fifteen months. Catherine had a baby girl called Mary, but

six days after the baby was born, Catherine died. After her death, Thomas Seymour tried to become Princess Elizabeth's lover. He was beheaded because of this.

King Edward was often ill, and he died just before his sixteenth birthday. Then Mary, Katherine of Aragon's daughter, became Queen. She was Queen for five years. She married Philip of Spain, but did not have any children. Mary was a strong Catholic and she killed many people who were not Catholics.

Next, Elizabeth, Anne Boleyn's daughter, became Queen. She was Queen of England for forty-five years. This was the time of Shakespeare and Sir Walter Raleigh. Elizabeth was a very great Queen, but she never married, and had no children. Henry married six times because he wanted a son – and he wanted his son and his son's sons to be Kings of England after him. But when Queen Elizabeth died, King Henry's family came to an end, and a Scottish King became King of England.

GLOSSARY

artist   a person who can paint and draw pictures

beheaded   when a person's head is cut off

believe   to think that something is right or true

bury   to put a dead person in the ground

calm   quiet, not worried or excited

Catholic Church   the centre of the Catholic Church is in the
   Vatican in Rome, Italy

cousin   the child of your uncle or aunt (brother or sister of one
   of your parents)

divorce   to finish a marriage

dream *(v)*   to have a picture in your mind when you are asleep

engaged   have promised to marry someone

forgive   to say or show that you are not angry with someone
   any more

God   the 'person' who made the world

great   special, important

handsome   good-looking (for men)

jewels   beautiful and expensive stones (e.g. diamonds)

king   the most important man in the country

kiss *(v)*   to touch somebody with your lips to show love

lady   a woman

look after   to take care of somebody

maid   a woman or girl who is paid to work in another person's
   house

miscarriage   when a woman loses a baby before it is born

mistress   the girlfriend of a married man; she is not his wife

necklace   a piece of jewellery that you wear around the neck

paint *(v)*   to make a picture with colours

palace   a very large and beautiful house, usually for a king or
   queen

Pope the head of the Catholic Church, who lives in the Vatican
 in Rome

pray to talk to God

prayer words that you say when you talk to God

prince the son of a king or queen

princess the daughter of a king or queen

queen the most important woman in the country

sad unhappy

sword a very long knife for fighting

ugly the opposite of beautiful

uncle the brother of your father or mother

view what you can see from a window

witch a woman who (people believe) can use magic to do bad
 things

worried unhappy because you think something bad will happen

Henry VIII and his Six Wives

ACTIVITIES

ACTIVITIES

Before Reading

1 Read the story introduction on the first page of the book, and the back cover. How much do you know now about the story? Tick one box for each sentence.

		YES	NO
1	Henry VIII died in 1547.	☐	☐
2	Henry was a good husband.	☐	☐
3	Henry's wives were all happy.	☐	☐
4	Many fathers didn't want their daughters to marry Henry.	☐	☐
5	Two of Henry's wives were called Anne.	☐	☐
6	Three of Henry's wives were beheaded.	☐	☐
7	Katherine of Aragon was Henry's wife for a long time.	☐	☐
8	Katherine of Aragon died at home with her friends and family.	☐	☐
9	Catherine Parr died before Henry.	☐	☐
10	In the Palace of Whitehall, there was a box of old letters from Henry's first five wives.	☐	☐

2 What happened to the first five Queens? Can you guess?

Katherine of Aragon	
Anne Boleyn	was divorced
Jane Seymour	was beheaded
Anne of Cleves	died after her child was born
Katherine Howard	

3 Which words do you think you will find in this story? Put a tick next to them. Why won't you find all of them?

princess	England	letter	photograph
president	horse	telephone	London
queen	car	gun	New York
pop star	tennis	sword	apartment
Italy	cycling	painting	palace

4 This story about Henry VIII happens in England in the 1500s. How do you think life was different then?

	YES	NO	PERHAPS
1 Could the King always do what he wanted?	☐	☐	☐
2 Was it important for the King to have a lot of children?	☐	☐	☐
3 Was it important for the King to have a son?	☐	☐	☐
4 Could women do the same things as men?	☐	☐	☐
5 Could the King kill his enemies?	☐	☐	☐

ACTIVITIES

While Reading

Read Chapter 1. One of Margaret's friends has helped her to write a letter to her mother. Use these words from the story to complete the letter. (Use each word once.)

handsome, necklace, letters, tomorrow, young, box, wives, tennis, old, yesterday, fat, hair

Dear Mother

_____ I went to Whitehall Palace with my lady Catherine Parr. We found a _____ with a large gold H on the top. Inside, there were _____ from Henry's first five _____. There was also a beautiful gold _____ and a piece of _____.

Catherine Parr told me all about King Henry. When he was _____, he was very _____ and he liked horse riding and playing _____. But when he was _____, he became very _____.

We're going to read all the letters _____. I can't wait! I'll write again soon and tell you all about them.

Your loving daughter

Margaret

Read Chapters 2 and 3. Which words or phrases from the story go best with each wife? The first one is done for you.

wonderful black eyes, divorced, beheaded, wild and dangerous, twenty-four years, three and a half years, Princess Elizabeth, Princess Mary, Spain, a witch, Henry's brother Arthur, six fingers, Tower of London, a sword, a gold cross

Anne Boleyn	Katherine of Aragon
wonderful black eyes	

Read Chapters 4 and 5. Then answer these questions.

Who

1 . . . could read and write in four languages when she was thirteen?

2 . . . was quiet and careful?

3 . . . was fat with a face like a big potato?

4 . . . died soon after her son was born?

5 . . . looked like a horse?

6 . . . painted a picture for Henry?

7 . . . couldn't speak English?

8 . . . gave Anne of Cleves the palace of Richmond?

Read Chapter 6. Are these sentences true (T) or false (F)?

1 Henry was eighteen years older than Katherine Howard.

2 Henry gave Katherine Howard expensive clothes and jewels.

3 Henry married Katherine because he wanted another daughter.

4 Henry was now very fat and ugly.

5 Katherine Howard had lovers before she married Henry.

6 Anne of Cleves told Henry about Katherine Howard and Thomas Culpeper.

7 Katherine Howard was a clever woman.

Before you read Chapter 7, can you guess the answers to these questions?

1 Catherine Parr was Henry's last wife. Why did she marry him?

2 Was Catherine Parr happy when she was married to Henry?

3 What was the King like at this time?

4 Was Catherine Parr kind to Henry's children, Mary, Elizabeth and Edward?

5 After Henry died, did Catherine Parr marry again?

6 Who was the next King or Queen of England after Edward VI?

ACTIVITIES

After Reading

1 Find the answers to this crossword in the story.

ACROSS

1 Katherine Howard was much _____ than Henry. (7)
3 Anne Boleyn felt like this the day before she died. (4)
5 Anne Boleyn and Katherine Howard died here. (5,2,6)
7 Anne Boleyn was beheaded with this. (5)
9 Holbein's job. (6)
10 Anne Boleyn sent Henry a _____ for Elizabeth. (8)

DOWN

1 Henry wore _____ when Katherine of Aragon died. (6)
2 Catherine Parr found these in a box. (7)
3 Henry broke with the _____ Church in Rome. (8)
4 Henry married six times because he wanted a _____. (3)
6 Thomas Culpeper was Katherine Howard's _____. (5)
8 Margaret's job. (4)

2 Do you agree (A) or disagree (D) with these sentences about Henry and his wives?

1　The King was right to divorce Katherine of Aragon. She couldn't have any more children and he needed a son. A king must think of his country first, before his family.

2　Anne Boleyn is the most interesting of Henry's wives. She wasn't a witch; she was just born at a time when women had to be quiet and do what men said. Today, she would be a very good wife for a king or president.

3　Henry only loved Jane Seymour because she gave him a son.

4　Anne of Cleves was the luckiest of Henry's wives.

5　Katherine Howard was too young to marry the King. It was terrible that she was beheaded at the age of twenty.

6　Catherine Parr was stupid to marry the King when he was fat, ugly, and ill.

7　It was more important for England to have a strong king than for Henry's wives to have a good husband.

3 Imagine that Mary, Elizabeth, and Edward are talking about their mothers. Who is speaking, and about which mother?

1　'I can just remember my mother's long hair.'

2　'I only know my mother from pictures of her.'

3　'When my mother was dying, I wanted to be with her, but the King said no.'

4 **Read this text about the life of Henry VIII. Can you find and correct the ten mistakes in it?**

Henry VIII, King of France, was a tall and ugly young man, who liked horse riding, football and playing music. He wrote many beautiful songs and had a wonderful singing voice.

When he was older, he became very thin. He had a very bad leg, and often couldn't walk. And when his leg hurt, he was always angry.

He married seven times because he wanted a daughter to be Queen after him. His one son, Edward VI, died just before he was thirty.

Henry VIII is famous in England's history because he broke with the Pope and the Catholic Church, and started the Church of America.

In 1587 he became very ill and died. His three children, Edward, Mary and Elizabeth, all became King and Queen after him. None of them had any children so Henry's family came to an end.

5 **Write a short text about a famous person (a king, queen, president, etc.) from your own country. Use some of these words to help you.**

was born in / lived in / When he/she was young/old
liked / married ... / had ... children
is famous because / died in / After his/her death

ABOUT THE AUTHOR

Janet Hardy-Gould is an experienced teacher and teacher trainer. She lives in Brighton, on the south coast of England, with her husband Geoff and two children, Gabriella and Joseph. She is interested in European history and chose to write about Henry VIII because he was an important king in England's history. Many people remember Henry VIII because of his six wives, but he also brought a great many changes to English life and religion.

All the characters and events in this story are true, except for Margaret, the maid, and the letters from Henry's first five wives.

ABOUT BOOKWORMS

OXFORD BOOKWORMS LIBRARY
Classics • True Stories • Fantasy & Horror • Human Interest
Crime & Mystery • Thriller & Adventure

The OXFORD BOOKWORMS LIBRARY offers a wide range of original and adapted stories, both classic and modern, which take learners from elementary to advanced level through six carefully graded language stages:

Stage 1 (400 headwords)	**Stage 4** (1400 headwords)
Stage 2 (700 headwords)	**Stage 5** (1800 headwords)
Stage 3 (1000 headwords)	**Stage 6** (2500 headwords)

More than fifty titles are also available on cassette, and there are many titles at Stages 1 to 4 which are specially recommended for younger learners. In addition to the introductions and activities in each Bookworm, resource material includes photocopiable test worksheets and Teacher's Handbooks, which contain advice on running a class library and using cassettes, and the answers for the activities in the books.

Several other series are linked to the OXFORD BOOKWORMS LIBRARY. They range from highly illustrated readers for young learners, to playscripts, non-fiction readers, and unsimplified texts for advanced learners.

Oxford Bookworms Starters	*Oxford Bookworms Factfiles*
Oxford Bookworms Playscripts	*Oxford Bookworms Collection*

Details of these series and a full list of all titles in the OXFORD BOOKWORMS LIBRARY can be found in the *Oxford English* catalogues. A selection of titles from the OXFORD BOOKWORMS LIBRARY can be found on the next pages.

BOOKWORMS • TRUE STORIES • STAGE 2

The Love of a King

PETER DAINTY

All he wanted to do was to marry the woman he loved. But his country said 'No!'

He was Edward VIII, King of Great Britain, King of India, King of Australia, and King of thirty-nine other countries. And he loved the wrong woman.

She was beautiful and she loved him – but she was already married to another man.

It was a love story that shook the world. The King had to choose: to be King, or to have love . . . and leave his country, never to return.

BOOKWORMS • TRUE STORIES • STAGE 2

William Shakespeare

JENNIFER BASSETT

William Shakespeare. Born April 1564, at Stratford-upon-Avon. Died April 1616. Married Anne Hathaway: two daughters, one son. Actor, poet, famous playwright. Wrote nearly forty plays.

But what was he like as a man? What did he think about when he rode into London for the first time . . . or when he was writing his plays *Hamlet* and *Romeo and Juliet* . . . or when his only son died?

We know the facts of his life, but we can only guess at his hopes, his fears, his dreams.

BOOKWORMS • TRUE STORIES • STAGE 2

Grace Darling

TIM VICARY

All they could hear was the wind, and the waves crashing on to the rocks. All they could see was the night. They could not see the ship, broken in two. They could not see the people holding on to the dark wet rock, slowly dying of cold. And they could not hear the cries for help – only the wind.

How could they save the people on the rock? Was their wooden boat stronger than the iron ship? Were a man and his daughter stronger than the great waves that broke the ship in two?

The *Forfarshire* was wrecked off the north-east coast of England in 1838. This is the true story of Grace Darling – a girl who became a famous heroine on that stormy night.

BOOKWORMS • CLASSICS • STAGE 2

Robinson Crusoe

DANIEL DEFOE

Retold by Diane Mowat

'I often walked along the shore, and one day I saw something in the sand. I went over to look at it more carefully . . . It was a footprint – the footprint of a man!'

In 1659 Robinson Crusoe was shipwrecked on a small island off the coast of South America. After fifteen years alone, he suddenly learns that there is another person on the island. But will this man be a friend – or an enemy?

BOOKWORMS • HUMAN INTEREST • STAGE 2

Stories from the Five Towns

ARNOLD BENNETT

Retold by Nick Bullard

Arnold Bennett is famous for his stories about the Five Towns and the people who live there. They look and sound just like other people, and, like all of us, sometimes they do some very strange things. There's Sir Jee, who is a rich businessman. So why is he making a plan with a burglar? Then there is Toby Hall. Why does he decide to visit Number 11 Child Row, and who does he find there? And then there are the Hessian brothers and Annie Emery – and the little problem of twelve thousand pounds.

BOOKWORMS • TRUE STORIES • STAGE 3

The Brontë Story

TIM VICARY

On a September day in 1821, in the church of a Yorkshire village, a man and six children stood around a grave. They were burying a woman: the man's wife, the children's mother. The children were all very young, and within a few years the two oldest were dead, too.

Close to the wild beauty of the Yorkshire moors, the father brought up his young family. Who had heard of the Brontës of Haworth then? Branwell died while he was still a young man, but the three sisters who were left had an extraordinary gift. They could write marvellous stories – *Jane Eyre*, *Wuthering Heights*, *The Tenant of Wildfell Hall* . . . But Charlotte, Emily, and Anne Brontë did not live to grow old or to enjoy their fame. Only their father was left, alone with his memories.